Luke 15:11–32 for Children

Written by Becky Lockhart Kearns
Illustrated by Corbin Hillam

ARCH ® Books
Copyright © 1996 Concordia Publishing House
3558 S. Jefferson Avenue, St. Louis, MO 63118-3968
Manufactured in the United States of America

There once was a father who had two sons;
  He loved them so dearly, each one.
The younger son said to his father one day,
  "I want to live by myself and have fun.

"Please give me my portion of money today
  That you have been saving for me.
And then I will go far away from this place,
  For I feel a great need to be free."

So the father divided the money he had;
    He gave the young son his fair share.
As the young man set off to a faraway land,
    His father stood in silent prayer.

The young man was finally off on his own;
    He lived wild and crazy each day!
But before too long his money was gone;
    He would have to find work right away.

Jobs were scarce, and friends were too,
    For a famine had spread far and wide.
The young boy was lonely, hungry, and scared;
    He had lost every bit of his pride.

He tried to look hard for just the right job,
    A job where the pay would be high.
But the only job that was open to him
    Was feeding some pigs in their sty.

The pig sty was muddy, smelly, and gross!
The pig food—disgusting and slimy!
The young boy was covered from head to toe;
He was dirty, filthy, and grimy.

He was so hungry! He wanted some food.
Even pig slop would be a big treat.
But no one cared for this hungry young boy.
No one gave him a morsel to eat.

He fed the pigs day in and day out,
　　Never having any food of his own.
His belly was empty; he was lonely and sad.
　　All he wanted to do was go home.

He thought of the hired servants back home—
　　"They have plenty of food to spare!
And here I am starving in this faraway land.
　　Oh, how I wish I were there!"

"I know what I'll do!" he suddenly said.
"I'll return to my father's home.
I'll beg his forgiveness and apologize
For the terrible things I have done.

"I will say to my wonderful father,
        'I have sinned against heaven and you.
I am no longer worthy to be called your son;
        I'll be your servant, faithful and true.'"

So he got up and went home to his father;
    For he no longer wanted to roam.
His father saw him a long way off,
    And he ran out to welcome him home.

His father was filled with compassion;
    He had missed his boy right from the start.
As he eagerly hugged and kissed his son,
    Joy replaced all the pain in his heart.

"Oh, Father," the young man said as he wept,
  "I have sinned against heaven and you!
I am no longer worthy to be called your son;
  I'll be your servant, faithful and true."

But the father shouted out to his servants,
  "Bring the best ring and robe you can find!
Bring the fatted calf, and we'll celebrate;
  For my son, who was dead, is alive!"

The older son saw what was happening.
He said, "Father, what's going on?
You never gave *me* a party like this,
And I've been your faithful son!"

"My son," said the father to his older boy,
    "You'll always be here with me.
And whatever I have is yours as well;
    You've been as faithful as you can be.

"But for now, let's rejoice together,
    For my joy and my gladness abound!
Your brother was dead but now is alive—
    Once was lost, but now he is found!"

Dear Parents:

At one time or another we can cast ourselves in all of the roles in the prodigal son story. We sin and stray from God daily. We catch ourselves grumbling like the older son, "Why can't I get the good stuff for a change. I'm not a bad sort." And in our role as a loving parent, we often forgive a child who has strayed from our direction.

God plays only one role. He is the forgiving Father—dismayed when we sin, loving us enough to have sacrificed His only Son to take our punishment, welcoming us back with loving arms, and hosting a party for the angels when we repent.

Model God's love and forgiveness with your child. Use the words "I'm sorry" and "I forgive you" often in your home. Plan a family celebration to thank God for His love and forgiveness.

The Editor